P9-DCU-918

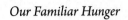

Our Familiar Hunger

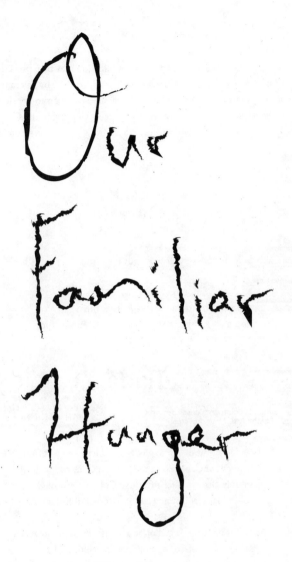

Our Familiar Hunger

LAISHA ROSNAU

NIGHTWOOD EDITIONS | 2018

Nightwood Editions
P.O. Box 1779
Gibsons, BC VON 1V0
Canada
www.nightwoodeditions.com

EDITOR: Amber McMillan
COVER DESIGN: Angela Yen
COVER & INTERIOR ILLUSTRATION: Shutterstock
TYPESETTING: Carleton Wilson

Canadä

 Canada Council   Conseil des Arts
for the Arts   du Canada

 BRITISH COLUMBIA
ARTS COUNCIL
An agency of the Province of British Columbia

Nightwood Editions acknowledges financial support from the Government of Canada and the Canada Council for the Arts, and from the Province of British Columbia through the British Columbia Arts Council and the Book Publisher's Tax Credit.

This book has been produced on 100% post-consumer recycled, ancient-forest-free paper, processed chlorine-free and printed with vegetable-based dyes.

Printed and bound in Canada.

CIP data available from Library and Archives Canada.

ISBN 978-0-88971-344-4

for Nelli, Lorna, Amalia

Contents

THEY TEST THE BONES

The Last Best West: Three Promotional Posters

1.

Free 160 acres of farmland
in western Canada! Homes
for everyone, easy to reach.
Nothing to fear. Protected
by government.

Wheat land, land for mixed
farming, land for raising cattle.

Rich virgin soil.

Westward the star of the Empire
makes its way.
This is your opportunity.

Why not embrace it?

2.

The country for agriculturalists!
Free grants of land, good wages,
cheap provisions, light taxes,
free schools.

Assisted passages are granted
by the Government of Canada
to farm labourers, domestic servants,

and others.

3.

Why? Because no other country offers
anything like it—a free farm,

a fine climate, a fair charge

for every man.

Castle Mountain, Canada

The posters promised farms, fields
stencilled yellow against the stamp
of sky burning blue. Red barn,
woman in white, dress licked by wind,
baby on one arm, the other raised in salute
to a man imagined beyond the page.

We'd not seen picture books, our own
stories not illustrated but told, but we were
lured by drawings like children. Tricked.
We came and they took the men away
from prairies surging with long grasses
and into mountains of bald-faced rock—
replaced unbroken horizons with wire,

gave them shovels and demanded
they tunnel into rock until roads appeared,
which would lead to peaks so beautiful
they would be renamed *castles*—national
treasures—and our men would be released,
brittle as split rock and sent, not home,
but to the prairie where our own skin
was cracked, soles of feet as thick as leather.

We became hardy with absence and when
they returned, we danced and sang,
our throats raw with gratitude
as curdled as the milk we'd make into cream,
sucked off spoons, our lips closed around
the taste, mouths silent against words.

What we didn't say: we were the women
from the posters, waving goodbye with babies
plump in our arms, chicken fat at our feet,
men unseen beyond the edge of the picture.
The wind always bracing, clean.

Beast Against the Yoke

We can't remember if we made it up,
the bit about our grandparents' early years
on the prairie, how they were so poor
they couldn't afford a horse to pull the plough
so Baba filled the part, acted as beast
against the yoke, furrowed the stony plain
with her own heat and muscle.

Imagine the will to keep going, clear the land
of rock and tree then seed rows with boot soles
worn of ridges, turning dirt like dull spades.
To watch crops of baptismal certificates,
high school diplomas, university degrees,
marriage and birth announcements split
ground and sprout. See how the next yields
broke the surface already printed on Kodak paper,
framed and placed on the dresser, gleaming
and scented with lemon balm, the grained
wood as rich as newly wrought earth.

We helped Gedo make his cigarettes,
the rolling papers pealed from the bark
of his limbs, tobacco sprouted from his beard
then Baba would say *Come* and lead us
into the master bedroom, lift a flowered tin
from the dresser. We knew what was inside—
the very best kind of cookies: store-bought.
She placed them on our palms like communion
and we knew it pleased her to offer us confectionary
made by someone else after a lifetime of giving
each of us her body, piece by perfect piece.

Stupid Hope

Baba preached about cutting hoes
against fallow land, tossing seeds
in frost, of watering dry ground
with tears so bitter they burn.

I allow my thoughts the weight
of clouds leaden with autumn or, say,
come up with spring, gold instead
of grief. It's the story I tell.

I will become good at a shy smile,
hum as I sway against the dark,
then hold fast, unwaver, unravel,
enliven until the pain is gone.

I'm going to believe in flowers
unfolding between the flinty crags
of mountains as I bear this dread,
these loads, as I refrain with ditties,

lousy with lullabies against
the long dark. I won't close my eyes.
I'll smile instead, hopeless
with the clamour of this stupid hope

that silence is the best I can do.
It's not as if we don't speak the same
language; we do. It's that not talking
is easier. Lately, as quiet as I am,

there's the sound of the train,
weltering across prairie, the scream
of its whistle, the rumbling underfoot
long after it's gone.

They Test the Bones

Reduced to exhaustion and anxiety
so distilled it's like a drug,
though this is the opposite of an elixir.

No tonic, if they steep their children
in this mixture, or place it under
their tongues, it will not inoculate them

against fear, but placate them with a tincture
of false courage, the brew both placebo
and poison at once, but no cure.

They test their bones against the strength
of old visions, wake to rows of rough benches,
the tables empty of food.

To their wives taken from their sleep-
warmed sides by the smooth hands of officials,
the smell of tobacco staining their skin

when they return. They wake to their children,
cutting their teeth on the ragged edges
of rations, playing with empty tins.

They test the bone cage around their hearts.
They test the bone helmet around their minds.
They test themselves and find everything wanting.

Others might be undone by the work,
frozen hulks of lumber peeled by hand,
cold stitching each finger, foot and limb first

with pain then tied off in knots of unfeeling
until there is nothing but bad weather
and more wood, more work.

Others might be undone, but they are not.
Shrouded in thin air, thick-skinned,
they hold tight the ability to forget

over and over each morning, each night
another chance to plumb water or sky,
nothing to break their fall.

The last thing they recall before waking
is the taste of their wives' blood in their mouths.
How the women bit their own lips to keep quiet

during childbirth. How they bent to lick
their faces as though they were animals
birthing their common litters.

Our National Parks

Baba laughed when we suggested camping,
the Rockies peaked with our hopes of clear minds
and sculpted thighs, our high, round behinds
as smooth as stone under glacier water.

Why you fools want to do that?
Your Gedo, he knew mountains,
he not want you to go to mountains
alone. Your Gedo he not want
you girls climb those mountains.

And we laughed in return—we knew
our grandfather had never been camping,
had never left the farm. What could he
know about our national parks?

Later, his name on the registry:
Banff/Castle Mountain.

He knew the mountains, his hands blistered
with them, the frost slicing off a finger.
He knew how he and the other prisoners lay
on ground near hot springs but never felt the heat,
waking stiff in tents iced by steam.

When it warmed and his bones jutted against
his thick skin he knew what it meant to be
on his knees, laying perfect sod over tennis courts
nestled in the crotch of mountains,
the ease the greens would speak,

how people would come from all over the world,
majesty ringing their vision as they lobbed
their balls over nets or spectated,
parasols shielding their eyes.

What She Carries in Her Chest

I write again and again about what she carries
in her chest while sailing across the Atlantic,
as though I can preserve in verse those apples
from her family orchard in Ukraine;

as though she can keep them crisp and juicy
even after weeks without light, banged up
on the dock in Montreal, where her name
is taken and she is given a new, English one.

I write for her fresh fruit that travels by rail
across the country to prairie pocked with stone,
heaved with cold. I draft the perfect shape
of ripe apples to share with her new neighbours.

I colour changing leaves as red as her cheeks,
her lips. I plump up goose down duvets, draw
a kind husband to keep her warm. And every
time you read these words, or think of apples,

she will hold one out to you. Bite into it,
break the skin. Will you sense the sweetness
and the damage in each soft spot, bruised
by distance; will you taste what she has carried?

Still Hungry

Our great-grandmothers were hungry
when soldiers barked from the jowls
of the new tsar and lined the streets
with tables, communal bowls on each,
told the people to feast.
                              What a shame

for the monarch when villagers were crushed
               under feet and grinding jaws.

Our great-grandmothers' mouths were not filled
with spoons of royal gruel. To celebrate,
instead they were filled with more seeds to
               populate the fields of the nation.

Our grandmothers were hungry
in the belly of boats that bucked them over
the Atlantic. They could not hold anything

down so they filled their heads with dark sky
above water, lined their stomachs with
                         the sharp edges of stars.

Our grandmothers' mouths sang songs
about the Old World and their hunger for it
was older than they were, older than anyone
could remember.   Their mouths gaped
with a time when everyone was well-fed.

Our grandmothers were hungry
when their new husbands were taken,
          boots pulled from the rutted soil of farms
heavy with stone and filled with the forced
labour of prison camps, while our grandmothers
were left to work the land on their own,
          till it unblemished, braid the dirt,

fill the holes with menstrual blood and pray
                         enough for generations.

Our grandmothers' mouths became
the mouths of our children,
                         wide open.

Our aunties' mouths left red marks
on cigarettes and the rims of glasses.
They held their mouths tight

in prim smiles for the camera
while their own mothers faced each lens
with still-faced stoicism.

Our mothers were hungry for the New World,
for miniskirts and hot rods, riding
with the top down, music tonguing the air.

They were hungry for university classes,
public transit, rooms in the basements
of relatives in the city.

Our cousins were hungry for something more,

something less than their hips tight
against jeaned pockets, their waists round
over the tops of tight skirts.

Their mouths wiped clean over and over
after the nights they held cocks
away from their teeth and thought
of the Carpathians flushed with spring flowers.

Our sisters were hungry for promotion,
their mouths smiling graciously
when department heads gave them

one more committee to organize,
just a bit more work because they were so good
at remembering the food for meetings,

so good at making people feel comfortable.

We are still hungry when they tell us
to lean in, lean in further, to flip
up our skirts, open our mouths,

                              open

them wider. Our lips move over the words
and sometimes when we speak, we are heard.

Often our hunger is the only noise in the room.

Spirit Lake

There is no Spirit Lake, Mary. No spirit
like yours, we'll acknowledge that—
the sharpness of your wit so fine
that it's a point of light, a wayward
star. But the lake of your youth—
those depths that you cross
with the shuddering outboard of memory—
there is no place like that. We've looked
on the map, our fingers along every
blue line, the places where they pool,
the names listed. There is no place
called Spirit Lake. Yes, there is no spirit
that rivals your own, but your memory
has made a watered body of grief
and given it a name. Your sister lies
at the bottom of another nameless place.
She must because there is no Spirit Lake.

CHAFF

The Tsarina

What she knows about me: nothing (everything)

What he knows about me: so much (very little)

What his family knows about me: enough

What they know about me here: so little (they call me the Tsarina, though
my husband is no tsar and my husband is no husband of mine)

What my daughter knows about me: (what I know about my daughter)

What I know: (only) this

Top Reasons Why Women Check into Asylums

They are tired
They are itchy all over
They hear voices

The voices are always calling them
The voices keep asking and asking and asking
No one can hear the women's voices
They refuse to speak

On the fall from bridge deck to water they believe they can fly and this conviction helps them not to hit the water so much as disappear into it and when they surface the asylum is the place where they draw a breath and open their eyes

They have shown aggression
They have shown aggression toward themselves
They have shown aggression toward their children
They have shown aggression toward their husbands
They have shown aggression toward their parents
They have shown aggression toward their in-laws

They have shown aggression a way to move through them, to express a lineage of aggression, to take the aggression of their family of origin as well as their spouse's family and to express it as their own then pass it on to their children so that they too can show aggression a way to move through them

They are excessively expressive
They are excessive
They are excess

They speak one language when awake, another when asleep
They refuse to speak their own language
No one can understand their language
They speak nonsense

They have been telling lies

They have told the entire village that the baby is not theirs, that the
baby belongs to the soldier, but there are no soldiers in the area and
this is very upsetting to the husband. They are not at war. There are
no soldiers. They are not at war

They believe the lies people tell them
They keep telling lies
They refuse to speak

The Air Was Filled with the Smell

The vegetables couldn't ripen
so we pulled them from the ground still green
and ate them, bitter and grimy as soot in our mouths.
We ground leaves, nettles, milkweed, sedges
against our teeth and swallowed until our tongues

burned and throats were ragged with pricks and pollen.
By autumn, henhouses were silent, no clucks or coos,
no cattle were lowing in the fields. Everything
that could be, eaten. When we went to forage,
we began to fall by the roadside and none

could do anything but roll the others to the side,
hunger curdled into an ache through our bones
as we bent to ditches. When the ground froze,
we were left like broken branches, useless kindling
in the snow. If we died in the house, we were dragged

to the cattle shed to lay frozen till spring.
No one was able to lift a shovel,
to split hard earth or hoist until holes appeared.
By then, there wasn't a cat, dog or sparrow in the village.
There were so few children left that the schools closed.

Our legs were swollen. Our stomachs too. Our necks
were as long and thin as cranes. When the ground thawed,
those remaining took the dead to the ravine
in ox carts. We pushed, six by six or seven,
and every second of us muttered a prayer,

every second slurred a curse, every third was silent.
We didn't add up to anything that made sense
and soon the dead outnumbered us,
ditches stacked with them, thick as winter hide
on a well-fed animal.

Chaff

after Hannah Calder's "Crow Circles"

The officer rips off a piece of bread,
still warm, asks me to open my mouth
so he can place it there. One chance,
or he will keep it all for his own children,
their tongues not roughed by hunger,
smoothed instead with cream, butter.
Fat tongues in their dumb heads.

I am not so dumb; I know
the officer likes the way
my face has been sculpted by lack,
how ridges of bones crest my cheeks,
my eyes set deep in green slurries.
He likes the way he can fill me.

If my mouth isn't swollen with dough,
the officer will shoot birds from the sky,
bring down hollow bone and soft feather
with the sticky weight of fresh blood.
He'll ask me to place them, still warm,
one by one in the sack and tie it shut.

I imagine birds picked clean, lined
on a spit, spinning over open fire.
Feel them in my mouth, salted and slick
with fat. I keep them from my teeth.
No teeth, I remind myself, just small
dead birds, hardening in the heat

then limp again, my mouth emptied,
stomach wrung with hunger,
soothed by the roll the officer leaves
when he goes, a bag of birds in one fist,
a bag of bread in the other, trailing
downy feathers, husks of wheat.

I Am Half a Breath

Noise and light explode
and we think it's the surging
between us, what we hold
under heavy skirts, but
it's another spray of gunshot,
another soldier marching.

We keep moving, sleep
on sheetless cots in cotless
rooms on woodless floors.
We sleep on floorless ground,
and not once do we complain.

We sleep in our own skin
and lie so close together
I can see how there is something
in the blue of your eyes,
as wide as sky pressed against
crops of wheat before lack

was steeped in pitted,
emptied fields, something
to omens we stumbled on
like sisters lost in the woods,
growing girls hungry for icons.

Please come and drink here.
I'll hold back your hair
as you bend toward the font
that once held holy water.
Lick what you can, a kitten
keen for milk. Our grandmothers

once lined these pews with boughs
of green. We'll garland them
with our bodies, arms and legs
draped, looped together,
the imprint of you so strong,

even the black bird of your
eyelashes settle, nests every
assurance away. Don't go,
don't go yet. I'll put my mouth
to yours, breathe into you;
I'll pour myself down your gullet

and disappear so you can stay,
so half a breath gets stuck
in my throat, not yours.
There's half a breath from me to you.
There's half a step to your lips.

Before Dinner

I'm back with the high ache of blue
above me and the pulse
of wheat fields shuddering.

My mother's hands hold my wrists,
guide my hands under the spit
of water from our outdoor pump.

How long it takes to wash the blood
of slaughtered chickens from me
when the pressure is so weak.

No soap, just lye and butter.
My hands raw with cold, greased
with salt and fat, held up

to the sun to dry
like featherless birds, wings
fingering the sky.

The Carpathians

What if day comes again and again,
repeatedly? If it keeps cutting into night,
splitting it open—not a round bowl
of sun but a serration of light?

When we sleep, hours open into sweet
clearings, mountains, a ring of high stone
and thick green, our bodies wide open,
five-pointed, nodding Stars of Bethlehem.

We are allotted sleep from mid-morning
to early afternoon, given naps later if we lose
the window to client relations. Never too much
rest—enough that we look fresh, that the mountains

circle our vision, leave our skin smelling
of foxglove and honey lily. Enough that we still
believe one more round of mounded flesh
will ride us from this tundra, back home.

Let's Call It

Let's call it a day, call each of us
imposters, our names Tatiana, Maria, Olga,
Anastasia or Franziska; Eugenia, Eleonora,
Natalya or Nadezhda. Let's call ourselves out,
call each other more often. Let's call
ourselves whatever we choose,
then change our minds.

Let's appear on bridge decks about to jump,
or mid-fall, our bodies weighted with air.
Let's appear in hospital beds and psych wards
and while we're there let's not say anything,
except when we do and then let's talk
about what we believe to be true,
or whatever we please. Let's manage
to speak and say nothing at all.

Let's sleep with soldiers who grant us
exit from one place, entrance into others.
Let's allow the children they plant
in us to be set afloat on curled leaves
held up with masts of twigs.

Let's accept invitations and take up
with dowagers, lower-tiered royals,
composers and wealthy American
industrialists. Let's make an industry
of ourselves, or not. Let's rest
when we need to.

Let's marry men called Jack and George
and call it a day.

What You Feel Most

Lay your hand against my brow.
What do you feel most—
smooth skin or hard bone?

Am I like water, caught
on rocks, or a tree, rooted,
flowering, fickle

as seasons? There is nothing
unexpected about orbits,
the tilting earth, clockwork.

Change circles through us,
temperatures rise and fall,
regardless of climate predictions,

so if I lurch between grief
and joy, both slashed open,
sloppy with fear, consider

it all weather, the whole damn
universe moving through me,
my blood clear of metaphor,

but not free from you,
your hands wrapped around wrists,
ankles, necks, gripped on handles

of blades and pistols, fingers
jumpy on triggers and buttons.
You'll stain the ground with blood-

speckled semen while I shed
leaves like so many layers of skin
cast off from the sheets.

Dispatch from State Hospital Superintendent

When women are warring
against their natural position

in relation to the reproduction
of the species while competition

for social and industrial life
and the growing desire to avoid

any responsibility that interferes
with material advancement

or social opportunity is so strong
it is not surprising that we should find

so many disturbances
of the nervous system associated

with the bearing of children
or that these physiological functions

and processes should be credited
with the untoward results

which so often accompany
and follow it.

AS GENTLE AS
OUR DAMAGE

Some Girls

Some bite dimples into their lips,
the inside of their own cheeks,
take their skin between teeth,
chew as quick as they can
between dates, then run tongues
against the inside of their mouths
to feel ridges and pits there.

Others offer everything smooth,
brows unwrinkled, relaxed mouths,
their faces not slack, exactly,
but clean of any pucker of emotion
that might pinch between eyes,
tug at lips, rise up in mounds
of cheeks.

How do you like your girls?
Electric nerved, jittered
and uncertain, buzzing from within,
or swept clean, blank as cloth,
sheets snapped over their bodies
floating downward so softly?
We have both, we have more.

Opportunity

Her sister goes easily to the other side,
to officers and mess halls and rough wool
blankets on skinny cots. The Russians,
she tells her, don't believe in hoarding
resources, don't believe in scarcity;
No, no, of course not. She stays home
with Mother, cleans the wreckage
from their doorstep, stops her ears
with cotton wool nights so she can sleep.
Afternoons, she takes Mother
to the neighbours' apartment, leaves them
playing cards, the tea too cold
and too sweet to be good while
she takes the bus further west, seeks
an unbroken connection to the internet.
She posts her photograph, nationality,
measurements. Her beauty is not hoarded
but quantified, triangulated,
an invisible string around hip-to-waist
ratio, then hooked on trade winds
across oceans until it catches on the nail
of a man typing desire into the keyboard
and is twisted round and round.
When he tugs, she'll pull back, tight.
Her resistance will be formal
until there is a proposal, a ticket, a visa.
What she wants is a good opportunity
to share what little she has.

The Sound of Hunger

A jet inks a trail of steam above us
as it heads to the conflict zone.

We raise our voices, not to be heard,
but so our toneless hums can meet the sound.

What will we do now, tomorrow, next week?
Should we stay here, with Gedo, Baba, Mother,

our fathers already gone? Should we go?
We've been invited, have ways

out of this place. We each have cousins,
first, second, once or twice removed,

who know of ways to leave. Some promise
flights, others the upper decks

of boats, but we know their deceit climbs
well above our wishful thinking,

even as their hands grope down below.
Will we go with them, anyway?

Turn the corner of the page in the book
we were last reading, tuck in our sheets.

Will we feed the cat on the way out,
raise our voices to meet the sound

of the jets overhead, mouths rounded
with the yawn of mundane desires, unmet?

The Black Sea

As the next wave crowned,
the boat broke free of the Bloc's shadow,
turned its bow to the sun-crested desert,
duned. We were cradled in newsprint,
stories of our Motherlands' former dictators.
The bottle we passed was not vodka
but warm milk sucked through a rubber nipple.

We held our stomachs as we disembarked,
queasy with birthing ourselves
into a new world. They pulled our hands
from our waists, pushed gemstones to our palms.
Skyscrapers scratched a dry heat
and the wealthy dragged sharp objects
along our skin until we bled jewel tones:
ruby, garnet, sapphire, onyx.

Thin Wisdom

Sophie is the prettiest
of the sisters, the fairest
haired. At sixteen when
she begins to starve
herself, no one knows
why.

You have to eat, Sophie,
her mother tells her. Do it
for Gedo who went hungry
in the work camps.
You have to
eat—

for Baba who, when
left behind, put each
child's mouth ahead
of her own, could fill
no one's plate
but

kept them alive, grew
enough of them to adults
that they became
your blood. Please,
you have to
eat—

for Baba's family in the
old country, starved off
their land, crops stolen
by Stalin's horsemen,
orders clear, sacks
heavy—

No, says Sophie. *I don't.*
I'll have more
than my fair share,
take three husbands.
I'll lose the first then stuff
my body with the second,

get fat with child.
I'll keep the baby,
lose that marriage, too,
then the third.
None of them
will last,

but you can't know
this any more than I
do—I haven't let
any of them in yet.
For now,
I'll subsist

on smiles and flicked
appraisal of my clean
lines, hip-to-waist ratio
teetering on perfection.
I'll daydream
about my first

wedding cake, white,
heavy, mashed
into my mouth by love,
years before
I know what doesn't
feed me.

Without Question

Only idiots ask about higher meaning.
We question this day, our daily bread,

if what is placed on our tongues
is food or the symbol of a body, taken

for you. Will we binge on a city studded
with lights, or be lined on the road

from the airport, bare legs cocked,
as though we are beacons?

Will we be given a new world in slices
through parted blinds, squint

into the prairie at swaying silhouettes
of oil wells pumping the earth?

Will we be able to leave, take the pickles,
poppy seeds and vodka? We'll polka

out the front door with such grace
that we could balance loaves on our heads.

Don't pretend you won't like it.
That's exactly what we said before we left:

We know you like this, Honey.

When you spasmed, it was with both
pleasure and pain, surprised.

You bled more than we expected
and we have a lot of explaining to do.

Eventually we'll come back for what's left
in the fridge. Until then, take a moment each day

to reflect, not on the answers,
but on which questions will be left to ask.

Our bodies given for you, we try to sleep
simply, without question.

We Are All Anastasias

We are all Anastasias, all Natashas.
Some of us are able to be Alexandras,
but few shorten that to Sasha.

Our names need to be long
to suggest the length of a body stretched
along bedsheets. They need to have

multiple syllables, four or five,
to suggest multiple positions,
multiple feigned orgasm.

Not too many, though; the men
want variety and they want to feel spent,
to rest after their due has been given.

The men are worthy of pleasure
and we are worthy of our new names,
the push of consonants against

the ridged roofs of mouths,
along the wet backs of teeth.
Worthy of the slippery *s*, the *hushhhh*,

the *ahhhh* at the end. We are worthy
of all that. We came already
with the right names to find them sullied.

Odessa

Wind snags sills before the flare
　　of dawn, then calms. The women
have their eaves nearly cleaned out, sodden
　　muck scraped then drained away.

What's left clogs their openings,
　　leaves them sucking at air like clams
under wet sand, breath tiny holes
　　dotting a flattened beach.

Each of them alone together
　　in the clamour of early light.
They push their thumbs into mounds
　　of muscle on their palms,

pulse into the ache of hands
　　after nights of kneading sloppy
flesh, their jaws and mouths raw
　　with the flicked stench

of strange skin made real,
　　torqued on tongues and released.
The corkscrew of night sucking
　　down, round the drains

in the street, then they surface,
　　shored up on morning, speckled
fish, pale, their silvered gills
　　weeping with salt.

As Gentle as Our Damage

In the heat of her room, she holds
a safety pin over the flame then pokes
her earlobes. This isn't supposed
to hurt. She stops the blood running

from her ears, between her legs,
leeching out of picked scabs
on her calves with cotton wool,
toilet paper, kitchen rags.

The house is rusted with the iron
of her damage. She's a mess,
old enough to know it, young enough
to not know how to clean

herself up. *Here, I'll help*,
says Irina, her cousin, bathes
her in black market micro-beads,
smears eyelids, temples, collarbones

with glitter. Later she's tattooed
under the weight of a man, his pain
suckled at her boney breast. Mornings,
she'll bruise as gently as the sky.

What You Do

after Philip Levine

In the lounge, your legs are a glossy line from ankle to hip.
You know that this is about waiting, shifting from one
stiletto to another, burn of false light along your hair,
blur of short-sightedness until you believe your sister

is across the room. Of course, it's someone else's sister,
narrower across the hips, but with the same round shoulders,
the small smile that doesn't hide her willfulness, the gentle
refusal to give into daydreams of sunlight as she stands
through a night shift at Kharkiv Machinery

so she can shore up on high noon to study English.
Your sister knows verbs and nouns, nuts and bolts, conveyor
belts, not the doltish man, waiting ahead, belt unbuckled,
just to say, *No, not you* with a quick flick of his dead eyes.

You can hardly stand your love for your sister. Can hardly
stand her heavy ankles, blunt hands, that she was never
the pretty one. While she studies for standardized tests
and visa forms, you stand in line, know that you are
too dumb to know what real work is.

After Winter

I push windows against frames until they give
up, spit out splinters of paint on the sills
when they are finally open, the wind welcome
to round its great mouth, blow until the shards
confetti the floor.

I'll leave the floors unswept, close the curtains,
white and billowed, as round as a bride
at her shotgun wedding. You teach me
colloquialisms while oligarchs hold revolvers
to our country's temples until we spread

our legs like drapery and lie quietly as sounds
enter the room—car horns on the street below,
an errant rooster, always crowing, a shop radio
bleating out the news of the day, laughter
skipping across a playground like a record
from the archives.

I've heard the woman from the next farm
gave birth to a girl, premature, her skin furred
like a small animal. Perhaps the baby is mutant
because she opened her eyes yesterday
for the first time and cried, *Smother the sky!*
before she started to howl. I've heard the baby
is struggling to suckle.

Dear Sister,

After the snow melted, the ground was rust-coloured, veined with oil. Raspberries twisted out of hard-packed dirt like wire and the fruit was tight and black until pressed between fingers and then it bled out red. We are too far north for orchards but I thought that if I dug trenches and poured seeds from out of my mouth and eyes, if I mounded the soil back up, something might grow in neat rows, bust out in blossom.

I'll be honest, I'm scared to walk the fence-lines here, my fear equalled only by that of wide open fields. In both places I expect to find bone yards, or worse, a new carcass, crawling with maggots, split like a gaping smile, wet mouth laughing. I'm afraid too of how strange the sounds are from the thickets and copses around the farm. Last week, all I could hear was the crying of coyotes—not crying, exactly, but a manic, pained laughter, like uncle after too many shots.

Do you remember the aspen grove that scattered light across our bedroom walls, left them trembling? Sometimes I think of that light, how it moved like a reflection on water. Here, we don't have trees that filter the sun like that but we do have birches that sway rather than tremble, allow me to uncoil their bark. I swaddle myself in it at night while sour gas flares go off on the high prairie.

Love,
Your Sister

We Have Known

We have known all along what we carry
of those whose blood travels through our bodies—
span of fingers and limbs, or the curve
of an earlobe, peak of a cupid's bow.

We can display a fine skiff of freckles
along the ridge of a cheekbone, or hide
a spray of bullets that long ago
met their mark. We cradle all the damage

that didn't destroy—split lips, boxed ears,
mouths forced open or slapped shut, the lengths
our mothers went to protect. We will hold
all we can; the rest we will fight, go down

with fighting, nursing newborns with warm milk,
our breasts flowering over with scars.

ENOUGH

Be Aware, Meet Beautiful

Ukraine woman here! Pleasure awaits!

Meet one of the beautiful Ukraine woman now.
Step by step we will help you to find your one
and only soulmate from Ukraine, Russia,
also other countries (former USSR).

If you are serious to find genuine relationship,
each one of these kind-hearted, sincere, faithful
and romantic women has the same dream—to find
her only man, create happy family based on love.

Registration for men is open now!

Question 1:
How do you feel if a woman makes the first step?
Bad/Good

Click here and we
get started.

Thirteen

At thirteen, light bloomed
out the box of my mother's
window, explosion brilliant
for a moment, then obscured
in steam. Later, ash was twisted
with the silhouettes of metal.

There had been an accident,
officials said. It was fine.
People celebrated at a wedding.
Others dug in gardens, some fished
in the river as the water silked
around their legs, throbbing

with radiation. When I was born
a year later, my mother prayed
that I would be full in all the places
I should be, that I'd contain
the right number of everything,
not too much or too little.

At thirteen, daybreak split
along the fault of two centuries
and I rolled and shuddered each
intact limb along to the music—
I partied like it was 1999
because it was, and then it wasn't.

I was as full as my mother had been
with me. My groin seared
with something like pleasure, my legs
heavy and from my fingertips, sparks—
the ability to trace constellations,
mark waypoints in gaudy ruins.

Repopulate

We watch our country's funeral
on the television, count our paces
from fridge to couch, back again.

Our country's birth flickers
days later, spotted in weak pixels
from the screen. We are shown

where new borders will be drawn,
as though others can be rubbed out,
maps not torn with the force

of the eraser, balls of rubber blown
from paper so thin light is visible
through it, a filter. Later, hearses

circle the block and children run
behind them. We decide we should
make this less of a wake, more

of a wedding, tie tin cans to bumpers
like we've seen in American movies.
We're too young to know if marriage

can be conciliatory, constant compromise,
if this union will bring strength
or harm, or both circling the other,

wild cats wary in the ring of an outdated
circus. We laugh at this, the notion
of marriage as entertainment, caged

animals, a bow-tied bear on a bicycle,
lady hanging upside down, spangled
on the trapeze. Laugh 'cause we're young,

too dizzy to do anything but flop
to the couch, retrace our steps to the fridge,
drink to being poor sports, blur borders

between skin, dig in, root for the home team,
each orgasm a drunken slur,
voices always in a minor chord.

Safe as Houses

We visit the rich-people
part of the prairie and I see
how the houses are made to look
like churches built from entire forests
of peeled trees, grains glossed smooth.

Later, we go to the Rocky Mountains
and I glimpse how rich people are there,
pretending to be Tudors in plaster
fortresses, dark timber accents
lined neat as fences.

My new husband has given me
English novels to read and in them
I decipher queens, ascension
and revolt. I read about their soft,
pale necks, what throbs, gets cut.

He gestures to grand homes and tells me
that one day he will present me with this,
my worth, and all I can imagine is how
I will give it all away, curl around
my own beating centre,
safe as houses.

An Equal Match

He takes me to see the prairie shudder
in the sun, a river snake through grassland,
pond silvered with light, low blue-green
hills beyond. There is nothing to fear.

He tells me to be wary; all might seem
like watercolour now, but when the season
changes, I won't be able to outrun it, the world
fixed in white, black, grey, frost, steel.

I know nothing of this winter. Instead,
hear wind ripping through the field, rain unruly
over the wheat, a frenzy of horses pounding
circles into the corral, geese crazed above us.

What to dread: he warns me against the spells
electrical storms can generate as they tear
through the sky with lightning, what charm
is in the silence that follows, seeded into the air.

He tells me to bar the door from summer nights
in case light from high planets drowns the memory
of fiendish false-delights in every longed-for
town. But, really, what do I have to crave or fear?

I know these seasons are faithful, will swaddle us
in grey and gold. I have a place here, something
I possess, so if the land wants me, I'll meet
its curves with my own, press in equal match.

Pipeline

We flow from east to west
—by rail from Lviv to Berlin,
by air across the Atlantic,
hour after stale hour tattooed
with gaudy bus upholstery
across this country.

In a prairie city, glass buildings
rigid against the ache of blue sky,
we are taken to the salon, waxed
from brow to toe, scalps stung
with foiled chemicals,
feet rubbed raw, nails attached
then adorned with fake gems.

We are taken further north,
stationed in motel rooms rank
with the unguents of our trade,
the hierarchy of hair colour—
for every blonde, a bottle
blonde, for every bottle blonde,
one with hair as dark as dug earth.
For every girl from a country

where *real women know how
to treat real men,* there's a girl
from the reserves farther north.
That it's most often
the dark girls, the ones born here,
who disappear and we are as sad
as we are thankful it wasn't us.
North is where they send prisoners—
the oil forced out of their labour,
pipelines slick with sweat,

pulsing with tears. Here too,
of course. We suck those pipelines.
They'll pump money into our mouths
or snort it up their noses or both.
It's we who make sure the oil
keeps flowing—an important job to do.
They pay us well for it and charge
us in return, add to the debt
we already bear. It's a cycle, really,
as bloody and inconvenient
as our monthlies; as necessary.

Trade Beads

I found my way out, as though life were passing
fancy. Now I'm a sojourned wife, the answer
to a thick man's prayer. His thirst
first-hand, my desire invented.

When he goes away to work, I go to the hotel
lounge, where native women look me up and down,
offer congratulations for being bought
for the right price. Dark hair is free

for the pulling—but not for blondes.
You are like gold, they tell me, smoked salmon,
beads rolled between the pads of fingers,
traded for a thick pelt of fur.

When We Haven't Had Enough

When we haven't had enough of being hit,
when we haven't had enough of being licked,
when we haven't had enough of being liked
or clicked on, we ask for more, we put ourselves
out there, we put out, we are out for more.

When we haven't had enough of being stilled,
when we haven't had enough of being lulled,
when we haven't had enough, we'll open
toward you, sheets around our ankles, wrists,
our bodies spread into five points, like stars.

In Town for a Conference on Eastern European Relations

I meet my sister at a bar
and she shows me the inside
of her mouth, the sores and stitches
like the topography of a map,
though the colour is all wrong.
No green and blue to cool the mind,
just the persistence of pinks,
reds, veins of purple and indigo
—colours of heat.

She douses her mouth
with vodka and lemon.
Antiseptic! she says and splays
her arms wide as she explains
how celestial bodies orbit
each other (this is not
a euphemism, she warns),
the pull and push, exact equation
of distance and proximity.

But you are trying this out
as a metaphor, I say, and it still
doesn't explain our marriages,
or the ways they've already spun
out, may break apart.
She used to be so much fun, I think
as I belt her into my minivan,
head already too heavy
for her loose neck to hold,

legs bare, skirt twisted and caught
on the handles of her hips,
exposing stubble along the length
of her skin. I fold her legs away
from the automated *whoosh*
of the door closing.
I'll drop her off at the hotel
where tomorrow she'll present
her paper on ethnic divisions

in refugee camps in Eastern
Europe while the party
that is my life means I spoon
puréed beets into my baby's
mouth, run coloured plastic
cutlery along her chin
and lips like a tiny shovel
until there is nothing
left, until she is clean.

Rank

after Pussy Riot

Occupy this city—it's your kitchen, your bedroom.
Mop the streets with your orgasms. Don't pick up

after yourselves unless it's to lift pots as shields.
Pervert battalions of politicians while naked

cops celebrate reform: the new order. Vodka spills
down their throats, splashes in our guts.

We're doing fine, but those bastards will face
an uprising of shithouses, infections spreading

and the rich circling the block in their limousines,
blue lights flashing. I took some kind of nap,

but the day grinds on like brass knuckles in my silk
pocket. I stir the soup we'll carry into Siberia

where the stench of ferment will become suitably rank.

My Dear Blade

after Lesia Ukrainka

Why are my words not like bright metal
in the field, a flare between two sides?

Why not a blade against the neck,
the slack skin, bitter tongue, foul mind?

I've tempered these words, drawn them
from my breast where so many rested,

but it is my heart that I'll apply to shape
each weapon, a curve of heat and spark,

then I'll hang it up high on display
to gratify others, disgust myself

with my only defense, my dear words
dying in my throat, unused.

I'll groom my blade and imagine severed
fetters. I'll echo loudly in bedrooms of tyrants.

Other knives will join in, sharpen new days
against the steely voices of women.

Here I Am

1.

Blood flows through my clothes,
red so bright it has run clear
of the stain of all those hands.

My skin is caked with thick earth,
stinking with nutrients brought up rich
from the deep cold in my palms.

Why are my fingernails rimmed
in dirt if I am as pure and fertile as rich land,
not soiled as those who dig about in it?

2.

This town is so young, yet
already worn, the dust thick on trees.
Nowhere is there a curved lane,
scented with lilacs, no billow-topped
church, spired with a steeple, no garden

wall. But here is the wide earth
where all the wide streets end.
From here you can see the moon
rise while the sun flares out,
edging the world.

3.

Out back, where garden meets field,
I lie and watch the night come.
If I stay still the stars pass time
by tracking invisible veins
across my skin, mark me

as one of many,
wink at me as they fade—

Notes

The poems in this collection were borne of several years of reading, watching and listening to stories about the lives of Ukrainian and Eastern European women, both in Canada and abroad. I tried to note every influence and source of inspiration, but took out more stacks of library books, watched more videos and went down more twisting internet labyrinths than I can effectively trace.

Here is a very small selection of the books that were most influential to my process of writing these poems: Victor Malarek's *The Natashas: The New Global Sex Trade* (Toronto: Penguin, 2004), Louisa Waugh's *Selling Olga: Stories of Human Trafficking and Resistance* (London: Phoenix, 2007), Laura Langston's *Lesia's Dream* (HarperCollins, 2003) and Marsha Forshuck Skrypuch's *Prisoners in the Promised Land: The Ukrainian Internment Diary of Anya Soloniuk, Spirit Lake, Quebec, 1914* (Toronto: Scholastic Canada, 2006).

Some poems in this collection are in response to work by other authors, and some are found poems, taken from public documents. I'd like to acknowledge and thank each for the work that inspired and informed my own:

"The Last Best West: Three Promotional Posters" is comprised entirely of text from promotional posters advertising farm land in Canada's western provinces.

"The Air Was Filled with the Smell" was inspired by transcripts from testimony presented by Tatiana Pawlichka before the United States Ukraine Famine Commission in Washington, DC on October 8, 1986.

"Chaff" is in response to Hannah Calder's prose piece, "Crow Circles."

The last two lines of "I Am Half a Breath" are taken from Roman Kosarenko's translation of Hryhoriy Chubai's poem "When I Am Half a Breath."

"Dispatch from State Hospital Superintendent" is a taken in its entirety from a statement made in 1899 by Minnesota's Saint Peter State Hospital Superintendent H.A. Tomlinson.

"The Black Sea" was inspired by Tomas Tranströmer's "The Black Mountains"

"What You Do" is after Phillip Levine's "What Work Is."

"Be Aware, Meet Beautiful" is formed entirely from text found on the main page of the website www.UkraineWoman.net

"Rank" is after Pussy Riot's "Kropotikin Vodka." The lyric "I took some kind of nap, but the day grinds on like brass knuckles in my pocket," is theirs. I added "silk" to the pocket.

My Dear Blade" is a response to Lesia Ukrainka's poem "Contra Spem Spero."

Acknowledgements

Earlier versions of these poems appeared in the following publications:

"We Are All Anastasias" appeared in *Calyx*.

"Chaff" and "Top Reasons Women Check into Asylums" appeared in *PRISM international*.

"Pipeline" appeared in *Arc* as part of a special issue on End Times.

Earlier versions of "An Equal Match," "Dear Sister, "Trade Beads" and "We Have Known" won the Blue Heron Poetry Prize and appeared in *The Antigonish Review*.

"Chaff," "Before Dinner" and "I Am Half a Breath" were honourable mentions in the inaugural Pacific Spirit Poetry Prize.

"As Gentle as Our Damage," Odessa" and "What You Do" were longlisted for the CBC Poetry Prize.

A sincere thanks to the editors, publishers, contest readers and adjudicators of the above publications and contests.

My gratitude to the Canada Council for the Arts, which helped provide funding for this manuscript.

My big thanks to Silas White and all those at Nightwood Editions who have provided the editorial and publication chops to bring this hungry book to life—Angela Yen, the designer who made it look so good, Nathaniel Moore for being alongside, and especially Amber McMillan, for editing this manuscript with such heart and smarts and wit.

Marita Dachsel, Jennica Harper and Nancy Lee provided feedback, critique and encouragement in writing this collection—thank you. And to my fellow Spokes: Natalie Appleton, Hannah Calder, Michelle Doege, Kristin Froneman, Kerry Gilbert and Karen Meyer—thanks to each of you for helping to shape this book.

The biggest thank you to my family—my late maternal grandparents, Joseph and Nelli (Nastya) Proch, who immigrated from Ukraine and passed along their stories, songs, dances and indomitable spirit; my parents, Lorne and Lorna Rosnau; and most of all, Jonah, Amalia and Aaron Deans, who keep my spirit fed.

About the Author

Laisha Rosnau is the author of three previous collections of poetry—*Pluck, Lousy Explorers* and *Notes on Leaving*—and the best-selling novel, *The Sudden Weight of Snow* (McClelland & Stewart). Her work has been nominated for several awards including the CBC Literary Award, Pacific Spirit Poetry Prize, Raymond Souster Award, Pat Lowther Award and the Amazon/Books in Canada First Novel Award. *Notes on Leaving* won the Acorn-Plantos People's Poetry Award. Rosnau teaches in UBC Okanagan's Creative Studies program. She and her family are resident caretakers of Bishop Wild Bird Sanctuary in Coldstream, BC.

PHOTO CREDIT: Tracey Nearmy